To Dave

Thought this would suit you [as you]
have a great love of dogs.
Great little pics with greater meaning

Well done for looking after mum!

love Baz + Debs

GUARDIANS OF BEING

GUARDIANS OF BEING

WORDS BY **ECKHART TOLLE** ART BY **PATRICK McDONNELL**

HAY HOUSE, INC.
London · Carlsbad, California
New York City · Sydney · Johannesburg
Vancouver · Hong Kong · New Delhi

Published and distributed in the United Kingdom by: Hay House UK Ltd, 292B Kensal Rd, London W10 5BE.
Tel.: (44) 20 8962 1230; Fax: (44) 20 8962 1239. www.hayhouse.co.uk · **Published and distributed in the United
States by:** Hay House, Inc.: www.hayhouse.com · **Published and distributed in Australia by:** Hay House Australia
Pty. Ltd.: www.hayhouse.com.au · **Published and distributed in the Republic of South Africa by:** Hay House SA (Pty), Ltd.:
www.hayhouse.co.za · **Distributed in Canada by:** Raincoast: www.raincoast.com · **Published in India by:** Hay House
Publishers India: www.hayhouse.co.in

Book design by Jeff Schulz / Command-Z Design

Library of Congress Control Number: 2009928663

A catalogue record for this book is available from the British Library.

First printing, August 2009

ISBN 978-1-84850-120-1

Printed in Canada on 100% postconsumer-waste recycled paper.

FSC
Mixed Sources
Product group from well-managed
forests, controlled sources and
recycled wood or fiber
Cert no. SW-COC-000952
www.fsc.org
© 1996 Forest Stewardship Council

پر

پر

نیو

نیو

بل

بش

بش

بما

True happiness is found in simple, seemingly unremarkable things.

But to be aware of little, quiet things,
you need to be quiet inside.

A high degree of alertness is required.

Be still. Look. Listen.

Be present.

Bring awareness to the many subtle sounds of nature —

the rustling of leaves in the wind,

raindrops falling,

the humming of an insect,

the first birdsong at dawn.

Give yourself completely

to the act of listening.

Beyond the sounds

there is something greater:

a sacredness that cannot be

understood through thought.

Look at a tree, a flower, a plant.

Let your awareness rest upon it.

How still it is, how deeply rooted in Being.

Allow nature to teach you stillness.

Everything natural — every flower, tree,
and animal — has important
lessons to teach us if we would only
stop, look, and listen.

Just watching an animal closely can take you out of
your mind and bring you into the present moment,
which is where the animal lives all the time —
surrendered to life.

It's so wonderful to watch an animal,
because an animal has no opinion about itself.

It is.

That's why the dog is so joyful

and why the cat purrs.

When you pet a dog or listen to a cat purring,
thinking may subside for a moment and
a space of stillness
arises within you, a doorway into Being.

The vital function that pets fulfill in this
world hasn't been fully recognized.
They keep millions
of people sane.

They have become Guardians of Being.

Most of us live in a world of

mental abstraction, conceptualization,

and image making — a world of thought.

We are immersed in a continuous stream

of mental noise. It seems that we can't

stop thinking.

Just as the dog

loves to chew bones,

the human mind

loves its problems.

We get lost in doing, thinking, remembering, anticipating —

lost in a maze of complexity and a world of problems.

Nature can show us the way home,

the way out of the prison of our own minds.

Close your eyes and say to yourself:

"I wonder what my next thought is going to be."

Then become as alert as a cat watching a mouse hole.

You may find that, as long as you are absolutely alert,

the next thought does not arise....

I have lived

with many

Zen masters,

all of them cats.

Millions of people who otherwise would be completely lost in their

minds and in endless past and future concerns are taken back by

their dog or cat into the present moment, again and again, and

reminded of the joy of Being.

We have forgotten what rocks, plants, and

animals still know. We have forgotten how to be —

to be still, to be ourselves, to be where life is:

Here and Now.

The dog is in the Now

so it can teach you or remind you.

Be alert as you watch a dog at play or at rest.

Let the animal teach you to feel at home in the Now, to

celebrate life by being

completely present.

The dog is still in the natural state. And you can easily see that, because you have problems and your dog doesn't. And while your happy moments may be rare, your dog celebrates life continuously.

You just watch the tail...

with some dogs you just look at them —

just a little look is enough — and their tail goes...

"Life is good! Life is good!"

And they are not telling themselves a story of *why* life is good.

It's a direct realization.

LIFE IS GOOD.

The human says, "I love myself," or, "I hate myself."

The dog says, "Woof, woof," which, translated, means

I am myself.

I call that integrity — being one with yourself.

The dog has no self-image, good or bad,

so he has no need to play roles,

nor does he love himself or hate himself.

He has no self!

How to live free of the burden of self —

what a great spiritual teaching.

EAT. WALK. PLAY. NAP.

"The key to transformation is to
make friends with this moment.
What form it takes doesn't matter.
Say yes to it. Allow it. Be with it."

Oh, that was the dog's teaching.
I'm just translating it into words.

Allow your dog to

take you for a walk every day.

It's good for the body and

it's good for the soul.

Dogs emanate a goodness that people respond to.

One of the joys of walking your dog is that often people

come up to you and immediately their hearts open.

They are not interested in you, of course.

They want to pat your dog.

Dogs offer the precious opportunity,

even to people who are trapped in their egos,

of loving and being loved unconditionally.

They have been with humans for thousands of years, and now

there is a link between dogs and humans,

much closer than it has ever been.

So part of their divine purpose is to help us.

But it always goes both ways. Because by living with humans,

dogs also grow in consciousness; it is reciprocal.

Because dogs and cats still live in the original

state of connectedness with Being, they can

help us regain it. When we do so, however,

that original state deepens
and turns into awareness.

We don't fall below thinking,
we rise above it.

Nature will teach you to be still,

if you don't impose on it a stream of thoughts.

A very deep meeting takes place when

you perceive nature in that way, without naming things.

SITTING QUIETLY,   DOING NOTHING,

SPRING COMES,

AND THE GRASS GROWS BY ITSELF.
— Zen Proverb

When you don't cover up the world with words and labels,
a sense of the miraculous returns to your life that was lost
a long time ago when humanity, instead of using thought,
became possessed by thought.

A depth returns to your life.

Things regain their newness, their freshness.

What is it that so many people

find enchanting in animals?

Their essence – their Being – is not

covered up by the mind, as it is in most humans.

And whenever you feel that essence in another,

you also feel it in yourself.

Every being is a spark of the Divine

or God. Look into the eyes of the dog

and sense that innermost core.

When you are present,

you can sense the spirit,

the one consciousness,

in every creature and

love it as yourself.

Love is a deep empathy

with the other's "Beingness."

You recognize yourself,
your essence, in the other.

And so you can no longer inflict

suffering on the other.

You are not separate from the whole.
You are one with the sun, the earth, the air.
You don't have a life.

You are life.

The one life, the one consciousness,

takes on the form of a man or woman,

a blade of grass, a dog,

a planet, a sun, a galaxy....

This is the play of forms,

the dance of life.

We are ultimately not separate, not from one another nor from any living thing — the flower, the tree, the cat, the dog. You can sense yourself in them, the essence of who you are. You could say God.

There is a term, a Christian term which is beautiful...

loving the Creator in the creature.

ECKHART TOLLE

Spiritual teacher and author Eckhart Tolle was born in Germany and educated at the Universities of London and Cambridge. When he was twenty-nine, a profound inner transformation radically changed the course of his life. He devoted the next few years to understanding, integrating, and deepening that transformation, which marked the beginning of an intense inward journey. Later, he began to work in London with individuals and small groups as a counselor and spiritual teacher. Since 1995 he has lived in Vancouver, Canada.

Eckhart is the author of the #1 *New York Times* bestseller *The Power of Now* (translated into thirty-three languages) and the highly acclaimed follow-up, *A New Earth*, which are widely regarded as two of the most influential spiritual books of our time. Eckhart's other works include *Stillness Speaks*, a book designed for meditative reading, and *Practicing the Power of Now*, which consists of selections from *The Power of Now*.

Eckhart's profound yet simple teachings have already helped countless people throughout the world find inner peace and greater fulfillment in their lives. At the core of the teachings lies the transformation of consciousness, a spiritual awakening that he sees as the next step in human evolution. An essential aspect of this awakening consists in transcending our ego-based state of consciousness. This is a prerequisite not only for personal happiness but also for ending the violent conflict endemic on our planet.

Eckhart is a sought-after public speaker who teaches and travels extensively throughout the world. Many of his talks, intensives, and retreats are published on CD and DVD. Most of the teachings are given in English, but occasionally Eckhart also gives talks in German and Spanish.

WWW.ECKHARTTOLLE.COM

PATRICK McDONNELL

Patrick McDonnell's *MUTTS* is a combination of his love of animals and his love of the art of the comic strip. Created in 1994, *MUTTS* now appears in over 700 newspapers around the world and on the web at muttscomics.com. *Peanuts* creator Charles M. Schulz called *MUTTS* "one of the best comic strips of all time." Patrick has received numerous awards for his art and animal advocacy. He has over 20 books in print including the *New York Times* bestsellers *The Gift of Nothing* and *Hug Time*.

Patrick is a member of the national boards of directors for both the Humane Society of the United States and the Fund for Animals. He lives in New Jersey with his wife, Karen; the formerly feral feline MeeMow; the still feral Not Ootie; and a new best friend, Amelie.

WWW.MUTTSCOMICS.COM

We hope you enjoyed this Hay House book.
If you'd like to receive a free catalogue featuring additional information
on Hay House books and products, or if you'd like to find out more
about the Hay Foundation, please contact:

Hay House UK Ltd
292B Kensal Rd. · London W10 5BE
Tel.: (44) 20 8962 1230 · *Fax:* (44) 20 8962 1239
www.hayhouse.co.uk

***

Published and distributed in the United States of America by:
Hay House, Inc. · P.O. Box 5100 · Carlsbad, CA 92018-5100
Tel.: (1) 760 431 7695 or (1) 800 654 5126
Fax: (1) 760 431 6948 or (1) 800 650 5115
www.hayhouse.com®

Published and distributed in Australia by:
Hay House Australia Pty. Ltd. · 18/36 Ralph St. · Alexandria NSW 2015
Tel.: (61) 2 9669 4299 · *Fax:* (61) 2 9669 4144
www.hayhouse.com.au

Published and distributed in the Republic of South Africa by:
Hay House SA (Pty), Ltd., P.O. Box 990, Witkoppen 2068
Tel./Fax: (27) 11 467 8904
www.hayhouse.co.za

Published and distributed in India by:
Hay House Publishers India · Muskaan Complex · Plot No. 3, B-2
Vasant Kunj · New Delhi - 110 070
Tel.: (91) 11 41761620 · *Fax:* (91) 1141761630
www.hayhouse.co.in

Distributed in Canada by:
Raincoast, 9050 Shaughnessy St., Vancouver, B.C. V6P 6E5
Tel.: (1) 604 323 7100 · *Fax:* (1) 604 323 2600
www.raincoast.com

***

Sign up via the Hay House UK website to receive the Hay House online newsletter
and stay informed about what's going on with your favourite authors. You'll receive bimonthly announcements
about discounts and offers, special events, product highlights, free excerpts, giveaways, and more!
www.hayhouse.co.uk

ECKHART TOLLE TV

At this time of accelerating transformation, in response to what he calls
"the evolutionary impulse," Eckhart Tolle will be teaching in a pioneering new format:
monthly webcasts designed to catalyze spiritual awakening, foster community,
and provide clarity, guidance, and support. Now you have the opportunity to join
people across the globe to experience Eckhart's life-changing teachings.

As a member of Eckhart Tolle TV, you'll have the opportunity
to submit questions to Eckhart, participate in live recordings, view monthly
talks by Eckhart, receive weekly Present Moment Reminders,
join online group meditations, and more.

To start watching or to learn more, please visit
WWW.ECKHARTTOLLE.COM

eckhart
teachings

The work of Eckhart Teachings responds to the urgent need of our times:
the transformation of consciousness and the arising of a more enlightened humanity.
We organize Eckhart Tolle's talks, intensives, and retreats throughout the world. We also
record, license, publish, and distribute CDs and DVDs of his teaching events. In addition
to supporting Eckhart Tolle and the dissemination of his teaching, we are committed and
dedicated to serving the new consciousness and the awakening of all humans on the
planet. Behind the external form of what we do, and behind the business structure,
lies the company's and our true purpose: the union with the divine.

WWW.ECKHARTTOLLE.COM